THE GREAT DECEPTION

To Fight or Not To Fight

By
Josephine Fussell

AuthorHouse™
1663 Liberty Drive
Bloomington, IN 47403
www.authorhouse.com
Phone: 1-800-839-8640

First published by AuthorHouse 1/25/2010

ISBN: 978-1-4490-7728-0 (sc)

Printed in the United States of America
Bloomington, Indiana

This book is printed on acid-free paper.

authorHOUSE®

CONTENTS

To Fight or Not Too Fight

Are you better than me, or am I better than you? According to the word of God in Proverbs 28:21 (KJV), "To have a respect of person is not good: for for a piece of bread that man will transgress."

Don't let the enemy tell you to do harm to anyone, for know this: what is not of God is of the enemy.

"For there is no respect of persons with God" (Rom. 2:11).

So no, you are not better than me. Nor am I better than you. We are all equal in the eyes of God.

My fight is not against you, and your fight is not against me.

"For we wrestle not against flesh and blood, but against principalities, against powers, against the rulers of the darkness of this world, against spiritual wickedness in high places" (Eph. 6:12).

Is the Fight On?

What do we do when we are fighting the unseen? Do we fight or not? Yes, we do, for the fight is on. As children of God, it will be that way on this side every day until He separates us. We are to fight a good fight of faith. In our daily lives, we are faced with different situations, and knowing how to fight each battle we face is a must, for it will determine our outcome.

To be victorious in a fight, we must be obedient to God first of all. After we are obedient to God, He in return will give us the qualities we need to mature in Him. Let's start with the fruit of the Spirit, which are nine gifts given to us by God after we mature in Him.

"But the fruit of the Spirit is love, joy, peace, longsuffering, gentleness, goodness, faith. Meekness, temperance: against such there is no law" (Gal. 5:22–23).

1. Love: Even if someone is treating us badly, instead of sowing discord, we should show love. This can't be done in our own strength because the flesh will tell us to get back at that person some way or another. I write this from self-experience, for I have been face-to-face with someone whom the

enemy was using against me. With God's help, I was able to walk away from that person and show love.

2. Joy: Having to retire from work, I lost my home and my land. I remained faithful to God, for my misfortune was due to my mismanagement of my money. Though I wanted to, I didn't get upset with God. God showed me (me), and I still have joy because of Him. The joy of the Lord is my strength.

3. Peace: After God allowed the enemy to attack me by trying to take my mind from me, He gave me peace with myself. No matter what someone else thinks of me or tries to call me, I know who and what I am. I am a child of the King. I am blessed, highly favored, and saved by grace.

4. Longsuffering: I suffered for a while before God delivered me from the snare of the enemy. My body is not completely over the situation at this time, but it is healing and just doesn't know it yet.

5. Gentleness: I pray and ask God to help me to be "swift to hear, slow to speak and slow to wrath" (James 1:19).

6. Goodness: I cooked a meal and shared it with others, not realizing that it was my last meal for that day.

7. Faith: By taking my hands off of a situation, giving it totally to God, and believing in Him to work it out. Because if I am try to fix the things only God can do I tie His hands, and I am not allowing Him to work in my life.

8. Meekness: When someone else is going through something, I do not put my foot down or my mouth on them.

9. Temperance: Temperance is about self-control. It involves allowing God to stand up in me instead of allowing my flesh to stand up in me. For instance, the enemy used someone to work witchcraft against me. By not taking matters into my own hands, I am allowing God to achieve revenge for me.

What Do We Do When We Are Fighting The Unseen?

Fighting the unseen is called spiritual warfare. Just because the people we see are the ones being used, it is not them we are fighting. Our battle is with the spirit behind the scenes. The enemy doesn't care whom he uses, nor does he cares where he uses them, including inside the church house. I can recall being in a spiritual battle and looking for deliverance at a church I had attended. God let me know there was someone there being used of the enemy, and they were working against me with the works of the hand. What did I do? I relied on the power of God to fight my battle for me. Before going to that church, God told me to fear not, for He was with me. With God's help, I was able to depend upon and trust in Him to deliver me. The enemy works through fear, but God works through faith. I was delivered at the church God led me to.

"Thy word is a lamp unto my feet, and a light unto my path" (Ps. 119:105).

"[T]ouch not mine anointed, and do my prophets on harm" (Ps. 105:15).

"For we know him that hath said, Vengeance belongeth unto me, I will recompense, saith the Lord. And again, The Lord shall judge his people" (Heb. 10:30).

"Men do not despise a thief, if he steal to satisfy his soul when he is hungry; But if he be found, he shall restore sevenfold; he shall give all the substance of his house" (Prov. 6:30–31).

The word of God is a weapon along with prayer, fasting, worship, and praising God. I have learned from my experience one thing that we shouldn't do: rebuke the enemy. We are supposed to bind the devil in the name of Jesus.

"Yet Michael the archangel, when contending with the devil he disputed about the body of Moses, durst not bring against him a railing accusation, but said, The Lord rebuke thee" (Jude 1:9).

During my spiritual battle, I said to the enemy, "Satan I rebuke you in the name of Jesus," and that spirit left, but it came back. The more I said it, the more that spirit came back.

"And I will give unto thee the keys of the kingdom of heaven: and whatsoever thou shalt bind on earth shall be bound in heaven: and whatsoever thou shalt loose on earth shall be loosed in heaven" (Matt. 16:19).

We are not to bind each other, for our fight is not with flesh and blood. So if I curse you in return you are to bless me. And if we hire someone to do our dirty work for us, we are participating in their act as well.

This includes playing the lottery. One night my husband and I rented a motel room. The location was very close to the store, so before going to bed, I went to the store to get some snacks. While I was there, I brought a lottery ticket. On my way back to the room, I took the card key out of my purse to open the door. I slid the card key into the key slot. Then I removed the card key and turned the door knob to open the door, but the door would not open; so I repeated my actions. The door still would not open. I looked up at the room number on the door to make sure I was at the right door. I was, but I couldn't open the door. That was when God spoke to me and said if I continued to play the lottery, when I came to live with Him, I would not be able to get in.

Wow. Talk about a reality check. So I quit playing the lottery. Well, at least I thought I did. A few years later, I asked my husband to go and buy a lottery ticket for himself. Since my husband was doing the buying, I thought I would be in the clear.

Oh how wrong I was. After I started writing this book, God let me know I had been a partaker in that lottery scheme. By asking my husband to buy the lottery ticket, I had "hired" him to do so.

"Or else how can one enter into a strong man's house, and spoil his goods, except he first bind the strong man? and then he will spoil his house" (Matt. 12:29).

"For we wrestle not against flesh and blood, but against principalities, against powers, against the rulers of darkness of this world, against spiritual wickedness in high places" (Eph. 6:12).

"Bless them that curse you, and pray for them which despitefully use you" (Luke 6:28).

"Lay hands suddenly on no man, neither be partaker of other men's sins: keep thyself pure" (1 Tim. 5:22).

Do We Fight Or Not?

Yes, we are to fight a good fight of faith. As children of God, we are in a constant battle (1) with ourselves and (2) with the enemy. A faith fight. What I mean by that is, say that I'm trusting and believing in God for a new car and all of the odds are against me, but I trust and believe in God for that new car.

So I put my faith to work by going out to a car lot to select a car. The salesman comes out to talk to me, or I go into the office, whichever comes first. We talk about a car, and I fill out a credit application. The salesman does credit research on my application. Then he lets me know if I can get the car or not.

If he tells me, "Miss, I'm sorry, but we are not going to be able to help you at this time. Your credit score is too low," I thank the salesman and walk away. Do I give up there and get angry with God? No I don't; instead of thinking that the whole wide world was against me, feeling sorry for myself, and thinking God doesn't love me, I continue on until I get a car, because that might not have been the car for me. Sometimes the things we ask God for are not for us. Sometimes that thing we are asking for may take twenty years, or it may take less. We should praise God and thank Him, and we should remain strong in the Lord and not waver in our faith. God has his appointed time to deal with each of us individually.

On a spiritual note, God allowed the enemy to use someone to work witchcraft on some things of mine. Did I get angry with the person being used to deceive me? No, I didn't. With God-given strength, I blessed that person in the name of Jesus. I got mad with the enemy, and I went to his Boss and told Him all about the situation. I started worshiping, praising, and thanking God even more after that incident because when the enemy starts messing with me, I know I'm headed in the right direction.

The enemy is doing his job. The word of God says that the enemy came to steal, kill, and destroy. Now all we have to do our jobs. One of our jobs is to not let the enemy silence our God-given dreams. In spite of the things I have gone through, I must show love toward the people that were used by the enemy. God told me to love the people and hate the enemy, and I asked God how I could show those people love? He saw and knew what they had done. The Lord let me know that these things come by fasting and praying. Jesus knew that Judas was going to betray him, yet He allowed Judas to get close enough to give Him a kiss.

The battle is all ready won. Stand up and fight a good fight of faith.

It doesn't matter what the circumstances are. "Nay, in all these things we are more than conquerors through him that loved us" (Rom. 8:37).

"Fight a good fight of faith, lay hold on eternal life, whereunto thou are also called, and hast professed a good profession before many witnesses" (1 Tim. 6:12).

So if we are walking within God, He within us, we are abiding in him.

"I can do all things through Christ which strengtheneth me" (Phil. 4:13).

Even when we feel like we don't fit in the click or have the feeling of being an outcast, we shouldn't give up.

"But they that wait upon the LORD shall renew their strength; they shall mount up with wings as eagles; they shall run, and not be weary; and they shall walk, and not faint" (Isa. 40:31).

Stop trying to get man's attention. Get in the presence of God. Get His attention. After all, He is the only one who can do something about all things. Let us call the spirit what it is, for it is a spirit that is not like God.

"These six things doth the LORD hate: yea, seven are an abomination unto him: A proud look, a lying tongue, and hands that shed innocent blood, An heart that deviseth wicked imagination, feet that be swift in running to mischief, A false witness that speaketh lies, and he that soweth discord among brethren" (Pro. 6:16–19).

Do we love in word, or do we love in deed? Also you must know that love is an action word. It shows. Jesus loved us so much that he died on the cross. Wow, what a love.

The greatest commandment God has for us is that we love one another.

"Beloved, let us love one another: for love is of God; and every one that loveth is born of God, and knoweth God. He that loveth not knoweth not God; for God is love" (1 John 4:7–8).

God is love, and love is what we want. Looking for love, trying to be accepted by man, is not going to happen without God. The word of God tells me that man will fail me. I have found this to be true, even in the household of faith. Some would treat you like an outcast instead of showing you love, and we know that God is not the author of that confusion. The deceitfulness in the house of God shouldn't be there, but it is. We should know the unjust by their fruits. God is not pleased with this, but He will do the separating of the right and wrong. I will rise again. There isn't a power on Earth that will hold me down, and death can't keep me in the ground.

I know who I am in Christ Jesus, and I know whose I am. I am a child of the King. He is King of kings and Lord of lords.

God is the only one who can do something about everything, so His approval is what I need. God has a gift for me that will make room for me I will be blessed when I come, and go where ever He leads me.

"A man's gift maketh room for him, and bringeth him before great men" (Prov. 18:16).

Not man, but men. More than one man who are great men. Whatever gift that God has given us, he takes it and cultivates it. To cultivate is to develop or improve by education or training. For example, to cultivate someone who has a singing voice or to promote the growth or development of an art or love and friendship of a person. "A man that hath friends must shew himself friendly: and there is a friend that sticketh closer than a brother" (Prov. 18:24).

The friend that sticketh closer than a brother is Jesus. Greater love hath no man, no man greater than the man that lays down his life for his friends. I understand that every man, woman, boy, or girl in the world is not going to accept us as children of God. Those are the people we pray for and give onto Lord.

"Let both grow together until the harvest: and in time of harvest I will say to the reapers, Gather ye together first the tares, and bind them in bundles to burn them: but gather the wheat into my barn" (Matt. 13:30).

In that verse, I believe God is telling us: Let the children of the night and the children of the light grow together, and God will do the separating of the wrong and the right. If we continue to walk in love with God; pray daily and nightly in the first, second, third, or fourth watch; and develop an intimate relationship with God, He will give us the strength we need to overcome the flesh.

"[F]or the joy of the LORD is your strength" (Neh. 8:10).

God is not like man; henceforth, He does not form a different opinion about us because of someone else's comment. He sees and knows all. He knows every heart of man's motives. God knows what is going to happen beforehand, and He knows what is going to happen afterward. He knows our thoughts, even from afar.

"For the word of God is quick, and powerful, and sharper than any twoedged sword, piercing even to the diving asunder of soul and spirit, and of the joints and marrow, and is a discerner of the thoughts and intents of the heart" (Heb. 4:12).

Also, we can't be counted out by man saying who is to go to heaven or who is to go to hell.

"But the righteousness which is of faith speaketh on this wise, Say not in thine heart, Who shall ascend into heaven? (that is, to bring Christ down from above ☺) Or, who shall descend into the deep? (that is, to bring up Christ again from the dead)" (Rom. 10:6–7).

We are our own worst enemies. God is not going to force Himself on us. We have to decide upon which path we chose to walk. Take, for example, Adam and Eve. God gave Adam instructions on what He wanted him to do. God didn't force Himself on Adam, nor did He stop him from eating the fruit. He just wanted Adam choose and obey Him.

"[C]hoose you this day whom ye will serve…" (Josh. 24:15).

Walking with God

After we choose to walk with God, we are on the great side with victory.

"For the LORD God is a sun and shield: the LORD will give grace and glory: no good thing will he withhold from them that walk uprightly" (Ps. 84:11).

Greater is He that is in us than, he that is in the world. No matter whom God allows the enemy to send our way to try and destroy us, He will make a way of escape. The more real and closer we get with God, the closer the enemy wants to get to us.

"(For the weapons of our warfare are not carnal, but mighty through God to the pulling down of strong holds;) Casting down imaginations, and every high thing that exalteth itself against the knowledge of God, and bringing into captivity every thought to the obedience of Christ" (2 Cor. 10:4–5).

Whenever the enemy comes after us with negative thoughts, we should use the word of God and not our fists to defeat his lies. Using one's fist is a good way to knocked out and get "black eyes" in the spiritual realm or a bad headache that may last until God removes it, if you know what I mean. God's word should be our weapon. After we repeat God's words to the enemy, know that His word will do exactly what He says it will do. After that, we have done all we can do.

"Stand therefore, having your loins girt about with truth, and having on the breastplate of righteousness" (Eph. 6:14).

Let us not give into the things that cause us to stumble and fall, but let us know within ourselves that whatever the situation may be, God will work it out for our good. Although it may seem that there is no way out, give it totally to God and "[t]rust in the LORD with all thine heart; and lean not unto thine own understanding. In all thy ways acknowledge him, and he shall direct thy paths" (Prov. 3:5–6).

Glory be to the highest Lord God Almighty, and in all things, give thanks.

To Obey or Not To Obey

Let us choose to obey God when He speaks to us. I tell you from my experience that to obey God is better than sacrifice. My experience about being disobedient was a sacrifice for which I had to pay dearly. God had given me the gift of discernment, and being a babe in Christ, I didn't know much about this gift. One night on my way to my job, God asked me a question. He asked, "Do you want me to do it, or are you going to do it?" My answer was that I was going to fight—me and my big bad little self. At the time I didn't know what I was up against. I didn't know anything about spiritual warfare, and the only way I knew how to fight was with my fist.

Oh boy, talk about being a babe in Christ. I had to be a newborn, for I was so unlearned about this battle. I didn't know how serious the situation was, but God knew. I was greatly deceived by the spirit of deception, for I thought the man was my friend and the only thing we had in common was that I needed a ride to work and he was kind enough to give me a ride.

God was warning me about this man, and the Lord told me that the one I walked with his heart is not with me. He didn't love the things of the Lord, and I felt like I had to fight for God. I was going over to his station where he worked to help change his mind about God, but I was going about it all wrong, for only God knew what my motive was because I was walking in darkness. Instead of walking in the spirit, I walked in the flesh, big time. So on my way to my mission, God spoke again to warn me not to go over to that man's work station. I disobeyed Him by not listening and continued on my mission. When I got to his work station where he was standing, I couldn't say anything to him, for I was buffed by the spirit of witchcraft. Disobedience is rebellion, and God considers it as evil as the sin of witchcraft.

"For rebellion is as the sin of witchcraft, and stubbornness is as iniquity and idolatry..." (1 Sam. 15:23).

However, when He was ready, God delivered me. But I had to go through something first. I found out that I was my own worst enemy. I had been walking in darkness and hadn't known it. Since that fight, God has opened my eyes to a whole new level in Him. God doesn't need me to fight for Him. He is a big God who can do anything and everything. He make something out of nothing. So anytime God wants to move in my life, I am learning to get out of the way. The battle is not mine; it is the Lord's. He will fight for me. I need to fight the good fight of faith. By trying to fight for God, I had opened a door for the enemy to come in.

"...When the enemy shall come in like a flood, the Spirit of the LORD shall lift up a standard against him" (Isa. 59:19).

God has the authority because He is the greatest. The word of God tells me that the enemy comes to steal, kill, and destroy. But Christ came that I might have life and have it more abundantly. Yes, the enemy stole from me, but Christ has restored me. God has allowed me to stand and hold on to His word, for He said that He will never leave me, nor will He forsake me.

"For the LORD will not forsake his people for his great name's sake: because it hath pleased the LORD to make you his people" (1 Sam. 12:22).

"...We ought to obey God rather than men" (Acts 5:29).

The book of 1 Kings, chapter 13, tells the story of a man of God from Judah. The word of the Lord charged him, "Eat no bread, nor drink water, nor turn again by the same way that thou camest" (1 Kings 13:8). So when he left, the man went another way and returned not by the way he came to Bethel. The man of God knew what God had said to him, but he was deceived by another man who claimed to be a prophet.

The prophet told the man of God that an angel had spoken unto him by the word of the Lord and sent him to bring the man into his house so he could eat bread and drink water. But the prophet lied to the man of God.

The man of God hearkened unto the voice of the prophet and went with him. Then the Lord spoke unto the prophet, and the prophet cried unto the man of God, "...Forasmuch as thou hast disobeyed the mouth of the LORD, and hast not kept the commandment which the LORD thy God commanded thee" (1 Kings 13:21). But the man of God went back with the prophet and did what God told him not to do. On his journey back, a lion met the man of God along the way and slew him. For the full story of the man from Judah read 1 Kings 13:1–26.

When we disobey God, we open the door for the enemy. In my life, after being disobedient to God, I learned the hard way that I need to obey His voice and lean and depend on Him. I thank God for things that He has allowed me to overcome. It was a lesson well learned. Through it all, as I have sat thinking and writing, God has made me a stronger and wiser woman. There is an old song that God has put in my spirit, and it goes like this: If it had not been for the Lord on my side, tell me, where would I be where would I be?

"Which things also we speak, not in the words which man's wisdom teacheth, but which the Holy Ghost teacheth; comparing spiritual things with spiritual" (1 Cor. 2:13).

"Beloved, believe not every spirit, but try the spirit whether they are of God: because many false prophets are gone out into the world" (1 John 4:1).

We will know them by their fruit that will manifest itself, for a good tree can't bring forth bad fruit, nor can a bad tree bring forth good fruit. Love, joy, peace, longsuffering, gentleness, goodness, faith, meekness and temperance -- the fruit of the Spirit, make up the character that grows in a child of God over a period of time that comes from above.

"If the world hate you, ye know that it hated me before it hated you. If ye were of the world, the world love his own: but because ye or not of the world, but I have chosen you out of the world, therefore the world hateth you" (John 15:18–19).

Favored By God

After we learn to lean and depend on God in our everyday life situations, there are benefits that only He can give. One of those benefits is the different level of favor with God and man.

"But seek ye first the kingdom of God, and his righteousness; and all these things shall be added unto you" (Matt. 6:33).

Seeking God is something we do by getting in His presence, bringing our petition before Him, and casting our cares of this life on Him, knowing that he hears us. I am a living witness that He will answer prayers. There are so many times God has come to my rescue. He has rescued me from myself and from the snares of the enemy.

There was a time in my life when I didn't answer to anyone but myself. I did everything that I thought I was big enough to do, and I did it only when I was good and ready to do it. One day I got into a big argument with the guy I was dating. It turned into a struggle. I got away from him and started walking down the side of the highway. A Christian friend of our family saw me and stopped. He asked me if I needed a ride. I told him yes, and I got inside the van. Before he drove off, the guy I was dating caught up to us. He tried his best to get his hands on me through the open window of the van.

My Christian friend knelt down in front of the van and prayed. Shortly after I saw him start to pray, the guy I was dating suddenly stopped trying to get to me. He got into his car and drove off. I don't know when my Christian friend stopped praying, but when I looked over to the other side of the van, he was inside. It was silent inside the van for a while. Then he spoke to me in a peaceful voice. "You know what?" he began. Then he told me something that led me back into the arms of our Lord and Savior Jesus Christ; he told me that the devil was trying to destroy me.

It was as if a light went off inside me. I started to think about all of the things I was going through. I was in a bad relationship, and I had been in a bad accident that occurred while I was on the job. It was then that I realized I needed to make a change in my life and get some serious help. The message he had given me was true.

So instead of going to my mother's house as I had intended, I decided to go to church. They were having noonday prayer at the church I was attending at the time. My mind was made up, and I repented. I didn't go anywhere to get prepared for church; I went as I was. It was an emergency. There are times when we need a blessing right now, and I can truly tell you at that time, I didn't think about how I looked or how would others would perceive me. My mind was on getting it right with the Master.

God may not show up when we want Him to, but rest assured He will come, for I know Him to be a healer. For example, as a child of God, I thought I wasn't supposed to take any medication. I suffered daily from my injury and waited on God to heal me, but I didn't get any better until my family took me to see the doctor. Dr. M.J. asked me a question. He asked, "How do you know that God didn't send me to help you?" After he said that, the Lord allowed me to take down the wall I had built because of the things that had happened to me. I know now that God works through people.

"And Jesus answering said unto them, They that are whole need not a physician: but they that are sick" (Luke 5:31).

So it's okay to go to the doctor when we are sick because God can work miracles through doctors also. I am a living miracle and a walking witness to that fact. While we are waiting on our prayers to be answered, we should begin to worship, praise, and thank Him as if our prayer has already been done. His righteousness is our action, based on love and a relationship with God.

The Added Blessing

This might sound strange, but God will allow things to happen in someone's life in order to get a blessing to someone else. It is strange, but oh how true it is. For instance, let's take a look and examine what took place in the book of Esther, chapters 3–10. The favor of God was upon her, and she became the next queen. Mordechai, her cousin, displeased Haman, the prime minister, because Mordechai refused to bow down to him. So Haman made a decree to destroy all of the Jews. Mordechai found out about it and told the queen. Esther told him to tell the Jews to fast and pray for a period of three days and nights. Haman ordered a gallows to be made for Mordecai. After Esther told the king about Haman's plans, the king was angry. And Harbonah, one of the chamberlains, told the king about the gallows that Haman had made. Then the king ordered Haman hung upon the gallows, and he appointed Mordechai as the next king.

"For with God nothing shall be impossible" (Luke 1:37).

"[Be] thou faithful unto death, and I will give thee a crown of life" (Rev. 2:10).

Great Faith In God

My cousin had great faith in God. I'm going to change her name and call her Faith. Before she passed away from breast cancer at the age of thirty-one, Faith and her family would travel up to the North from down South during the holidays and visit with us. We were teenagers, but I was a little older than she was, and we bonded well together, almost like sisters. One of our family activities was gathering in the front of the house and singing church songs.

Remembering her last visit to the South to our grandparents' house, I can recall her talking with our granddaddy. I saw something different about her on that day. While watching her intently from afar, I could see that she was happy. She was so happy that I became a little jealous; I wanted to feel what she felt. I guess I was jealous in a Godly way, for I didn't want to bring her any harm. I just wanted to feel the happiness that was overflowing in her.

Have you ever seen anyone so happy and free, without a care in this world? Her spirit was so free until it flowed through her. I didn't understand it then, but I know now that it was the joy of the Lord. After she became sick, we traveled to visit her. My plan was to go and encourage her. After our arrival, I finally got up the courage to walk over to her bedside. Faith reached out for my hand,

and before any words came out of my mouth, she said to me, "I want you to do something for me. I want you to get saved."

At that time in my life, I was a backslidden Christian. But what great faith this woman had in God. She was not concerned with her own life; she was more concerned about me. I do believe that Faith had already made her peace with God and that she knew where she would be going.

"And take heed to yourselves, lest at any time your hearts be overcharged with surfeiting, and drunkenness, and cares of this life, and so that day come upon you unawares" (Luke 21:34).

Pay attention to yourselves lest at any time your hearts are burdened down with too much of anything and with drunkenness and with cares of this life. The second coming of Jesus will come upon you when least expected.

"Watch ye therefore, and pray always, that ye may be accounted worthy to escape all the things that shall come to pass, and stand before the Son of man" (Luke 21:36).

Not only do I believe Faith made her peace with God, but I believe she had the peace of God.

"And the peace of God, which passeth all understanding, shall keep your hearts and minds through Christ Jesus" (Phil. 4:7).

Within our bodies, our hearts and minds have to be equally yoked together. We cannot waver in our Christian walk. We must be totally sold out to God. If we get real and keep it real with God, He will get real with us and in us. I also believe Faith was accepted by God and that she had escaped from the cares of this life. Can you imagine how it would feel to know that you are dying, but it doesn't matter to you, for you have so much joy to know that you are going to live with God? I heard that she told her mother that she was going to heaven. She said it with much joy in her voice, as if an angel was speaking through her. I must admit, that is the joy the world can't give to us—knowing that we are safe in the arms of Jesus and that to die in Christ is a gain.

"I press toward the mark for the prize of the high calling of God in Christ Jesus" (Phil. 3:14).

We have to be devoted entirely headed in the direction of the spiritual reward of the Lord. "And this is the promise that he hath promised us, even eternal life" (1 John 2:25).

God Promised

"And we know that all things work together for good to them that love God, to them who are called according to his purpose" (Rom. 8:28).

After my accident in 1992, I was weighed down with the cares of this life. I realize now that God allowed those things to take place in my life for a reason. Before the accident, I had forgotten about God. I was not seeking His will; I was seeking the things I wanted and the things I wanted to do. I hurt my husband and others as well as myself with my lifestyle. I know I can't take those things back, for it takes God to mend broken hearts. We can only be forgiven; so we have to forgive ourselves and let it go.

That was one of the hardest things for me to do, to forgive myself and let it go. Being burdened with the cares of this life had made me a mean and bitter person. I didn't realize I had so much hate in me until God revealed it to me. God showed me myself, and with His help I was able to love again. The closer I got to God, the more He opened my eyes so I could see what the enemy was doing to me. God changed my heart and my mind from Satan's kingdom to His Kingdom. I am married with three grown children—two sons, one daughter—one goddaughter, ten grandchildren, and three grand-godchildren. I thank God for all my family members, especially my husband.

God showed me how to love again through some of the things my family members went through with. My daughter divorced her husband, who was abusive to her and her daughter. One night or morning, he beat my daughter in the eye and beat my granddaughter—who was not his own child—on her body. I didn't find out about it until later when my cousin called me and informed me what had taken place. My cousin had visited the location where the beating took place. She said that she knocked on the door, but my daughter's husband wouldn't let her in. When she turned to leave, God spoke to her and told her not to leave that child.

The police became involved, and that is how they were able to get my daughter and granddaughter to a safe place. I was told that my daughter didn't tell the truth about what had happened. At that time, my daughter was pregnant with her third child. My cousin took them to her house. It was there that I saw what they looked like as they approached our car. I couldn't move. It was as if I was stuck to the ground in the spot where I was standing. I had never seen my child and my granddaughter look and walk in so much pain.

On the way home, I didn't have much to say, for I was in pain myself. The hurt manifested itself after the birth of my grandson. When my grandson was born, I went to help my daughter at her apartment. While I was there, I found out I had a problem with the baby. The baby looked just like his daddy. I didn't talk about it to anyone but God. I don't know how many months went by before God delivered me from not wanting to be around and not wanting to do anything for the baby. The more I was put in the position of being in the same room with the baby, the more God allowed me to see the pleasant spirit and wonderful smile he had. Thank you, Lord for allowing me to overcome my pain and to keep my eyes on you and your promises.

- In Joel 2:23, God promised me a double portion the former rain and latter rain.

- In verse 24, He promised me financial prosperity: "And the floors shall be full of wheat, and the vats shall overflow with new wine and oil."

- In verse 25, He promised restoration: "And I will restore to you the years that the locus hath eaten, cankerworm, and the cater-pillar, and the palmerworm, my great army which I sent among you."

- In verse 26–27, God's presence and favor satisfied: "[A]nd praise the name of the LORD your God…and none else: and my people shall never be ashamed."

- In verse 28, He gave blessings for my sons and daughters. God said: "…I will pour out my spirit upon all flesh; and your sons and your daughters shall prophesy, your old men shall dream dreams, your young men shall see visions."

- In verse 30, there are special miracles: "And I will shew wonders in the heavens and in the earth…"

- And in verse 32, He promised deliverance: "[W]hosoever shall call on the name of the LORD shall be delivered…"

God's Healing Power

Sometime it hurts to love, especially after we have been hurt or been done wrong by others in any way. This is when we need to go to the Lord and come clean by pouring out of our hearts to God. We need to tell Him all about how we feel because He is the only one who can help—not to ease, but to remove our pain.

In any situation, after we have given our hearts to God, we have to let go of the things we can't change. He will move on our behalf. We don't know when he's going to move on our problem, but I promise you that you will know when He has moved for you. Those things that use to hinder us will not hurt as badly, and we will find ourselves tolerating them. Then we will start remembering the times when those things that hurt us were not there any longer. I originally wanted to go into more details about my accident in 1992, but I can't because I no longer have the pain, hurt, and shame I once felt. It's gone. But I can tell you this: it was not a car accident.

My accident happened on the job. I had to give those things to God and let go of them or else it would have destroyed me or it would have destroyed someone else because hurt people hurt other people. To God be the glory for the great things He has done and is doing and is going to do my life.

Along with giving the things that hurt us to God, we have to forgive in order to be forgiven. And to everyone that I have caused any hurt, harm, or shame, I ask your forgiveness. I know that I was as mean as the enemy was, for God showed me. I can't take those things back, but I am sorry for them, with Godly sorrow, Can't nobody reward you like Jesus To those who have labored in prayer upon my behalf, thank you He keeps on blessing, and there is no limiting Him in what He can do.

Those things God allowed to happen to me worked out to my benefit, for I know that He has a purpose and a plan for my life. Tuesday, September 8, 2009, was my visit to the doctor. I had my office appointment, talked to the doctor, and got my prescription note. After I paid for my visit, I left the office. On my way home, I realized I hadn't scheduled my next appointment. When I went to the pharmacist to get my prescription filled, I was told it would be approximately thirty minutes before I could get my medication, so I left and retuned later that day to pick it up. Upon my return, I was told that they needed to get authorization from my insurance before I could get the medicine. The next day I called the doctor's office, and I was told they had sent the papers off.

On Friday, I called the pharmacist again, and they were still waiting on the authorization. They told me that I needed to talk to my doctor. So I did. This time I called on Dr. Jesus. I told Him all about the problem. Oh my God, He is so awesome, and I am trusting and believing in His divine healing power to totally heal me of that illness. He can do it, but if He doesn't heal me, I still know that He can because there is nothing too hard for Him. It's a God thing. And it is a God kind of thing, for it is by His Spirit. I will be delivered by God's timing and not by my own.

I have since received the authorization to get my next refill, so I'll be going back to the doctor. I have been taking medicine for that illness for about fifteen years, but that doesn't matter with God. It doesn't matter about how long it has been for me to be healed completely. In the Bible (Luke 8:43) He healed the woman who had the issue of blood for twelve years. I am a firm believer that there is nothing to hard for Him, for truly He is a miracle worker.

"[T]here was given to me a thorn in the flesh, the messenger of Satan to buffet me, lest I should be exalted above measure. For this thing I besought the Lord thrice, that it might depart from me. And he said unto me, My grace is sufficient for thee: for my strength is made perfect in weakness. Most gladly therefore I will rather glory in my infirmities, that the power of Christ may rest upon me" (2 Cor. 12:7–9).

This was what Paul was talking about when he spoke of a problem he had in his flesh. He sought the Lord three times for Him to remove it. And God told him that His grace was adequate for the purpose, for His strength is perfected in weakness. Afterward, Paul became glad about his problem and that the power of Christ supported him. It's recorded in the Holy Bible 2 Cor. 12:7-9, so whose report will we believe the enemies or God's? I'm going to believe the report of the Lord. He caused the lame to walk, opened the eyes of the blind, and cast demons out of the dumb.

As for myself and my situation, I will remain joyful in the Lord and continue to pray, fast, read my bible, attend church, and trust in the Lord. I'm going to hold on to God's unchanging hands until my change comes. Weeping may endure for a night, but joy cometh in the morning. God has a purpose and a plan for me.

"For I know the thoughts that I think toward you, saith the LORD, thoughts of peace, and not of evil, to give you an expected end" (Jer. 29:11).

An expected end is God's promise to all who walk according to His reason and design for their existence.

A Design Appointment

Jesus is soon to return, though no man knows the day or the hour of His coming. Our job is to be ready when He comes. At some point in life, we all have had some type of scheduled appointment, whether we kept it or we made it. God has a divine scheduled appointment, and it is for the return of Jesus.

"Behold, he cometh with clouds; and every eye shall see him..." (Rev. 1:7).

"He that hath an ear, let him hear what the Spirit saith unto the churches; He that overcometh shall not be hurt of the second death" (Rev. 2:11).

At this divine appointment, everyone will be present to see Him, and this is one appointment we can't cancel. He that has an ear, let him hear what the spirit is saying unto us. He that is ready to go with Christ when He comes shall not be hurt of the second death. My belief is that Christ has paid the ultimate price—shedding His blood and dying on the cross for us. Those people that remain after the first resurrection will have to shed their own blood and die in order to get into the Kingdom of God. To make this personal, let all of us—he, she, you, and me—get our houses in order to go with Christ in the first resurrection.

"And it is appointed unto men once to die, but after this the judgment" (Heb. 9:27).

To summarize, know that we are all created equally by God and that no one is better than another person. The word of God lets us know that anything different than His Word is wrong. We are not to have a respect of person. Our respect should not be based solely on a person's possessions or background. For example, if my car is better than yours, I should not withhold respect from you just because you drive an ugly car.

There is nothing to hard for The Lord, for through Him all things are possible. He gave us His promise; He said that He would never leave us or forsake us. So in any battle we are faced with, we should know that it is not our battle. It is the Lord's battle. It is not about us. It's about Jesus.

Let us not love in words but rather let us love in deed, with the genuine agape love that only God can give when we seek Him. If someone tells you that he or she loves you but he or she never showed that love, you would probably wonder if that person's love is genuine. Love is an action word. Love will show you if it is true. Jesus Christ demonstrated His love for all mankind before the cross, on the cross, and after the cross, and His love continues in action for us all. We show our love to God by walking with him as closely as we can.

If we obey Him and do His will, He will show us His favor. God will give us favor, with added blessing. My cousin Faith, whose real name is Diane Roberts Anderson, showed me that Christ can and will make a difference in our lives when we lean and depend on Him. She was a living example of Christ on Earth for me. He will show up and bless like only God can. We have His promise that He will assist us in every given situation with His awesome healing power. He let us know in John 11:4: "That sickness is not unto death, but for the glory of God, that the Son of God might be glorified thereby."

My daughter has forgiven her husband and has decided to give their relationship another try; he has been seeking some help with his issues also. God has moved on my behalf regarding his abuse of my daughter and granddaughter, for the Lord has given me the chance to forgive him. After being hurt, sometimes we put up a wall of defense without realizing it. There are times when that means hurting someone else before they hurt us, without first realizing that we have a problem that needs attention before it gets out of control. Many times we can see other people's problems before we can see our own. I found this to be true in my own life. I frequently pray and ask God to show me Josephine). My prayer is that we are ready when Jesus comes and that we are not deceived by the enemy. We are divinely loved by Jesus.

PERSONAL NOTE FROM THE AUTHOR

To whoever's hands this book touches, to God be the glory. If these pages that I have written never leave our apartment to be edited, published, or marketed, so be it. I already have what money can't buy, and that is God's approval on the words that He has given to me to put down on paper. And how do I know that I have God's approval on these words? I'll tell you.

Did you notice the smiley face under God's commandment? "Say not in thine heart, Who shall ascend into heaven? (that is to bring Christ down from above ☺:)" (Rom. 10:6). That is God's seal of approval for me. I didn't type it there. God stamped that smiley face there. Thank you, God, for the wisdom, knowledge, understanding, and sound mind you have given unto me. I don't know where I would be if not for the Lord. For the enemy came after me so many times to try to take my mind from me. I did all I know to do, and that was to stand on the word of God.

"For God hath not given us the spirit of fear; but of power, and of love, and a sound mind" (2 Tim. 1:7).

"So shall they fear the name of the LORD from the west, and his glory from the rising of the sun. When the enemy shall come in like a flood, the Spirit of the LORD shall lift up a standard against him" (Isa. 59:19).

Maybe these words are just for me; the studying, the hours and days it took to prepare this book have truly inspired me. Wow. Imagine that: I even feel closer to God. Now I know that I needed to write this book, for this is conformation to a dream God gave to me approximately two years ago. His interpretation of the dream He gave to me was that I should share the good news about Christ.

In the dream, I was standing outside with my mother, looking up toward the sky at the moon. My aunt stood to our right, also looking up toward the sky. We asked her to take a look at what we were looking at. Then she asked us to take a look at what she was looking at. We walked over to where she stood and looked up toward the sky, and there was a cartoon character standing by a hole in the sky, and people were going into the hole. I was sad, for at this time I didn't go up.

Then, as we started to go into the house, some people from the news media showed up and asked questions about what had taken place. They wanted to know why we hadn't gone up. I didn't give them an answer, for I went into the house. Shortly after, I awoke from my dream. I asked God what He had shown me, and He said the message was for me to get my house in order and that Jesus is soon to come. He also told me that the cartoon character I saw was not real, but when Jesus returns, he will be the real deal, and the news media was a symbol for me to share the good news about Christ.

POETRY

This poem, "It Must Be Me," was given to me by God while I was surfing the Internet on poetry. I never knew much about poetry before that. I wrote down the title God gave me, and as I wrote, the body came flowing into me.

It Must Be Me

It must be me I can see soaring high among the clouds. Higher than the birds can see. High enough for you and me. It must be me, can you see, or is it you I can see? It must be you with me we can see. High enough, for we all can be. High enough for God to see. It must be me. I need to be. Do you feel the need to be? In that place where we all can be. It must be me I can see. In that land of liberty. Being free, as free as we can be. This is the place we need to be, you must see. So be carefree, for eternity, living there, you and me. Can you imagine you and me being free as free as we can be? Yes I can see it must be me. You and me, can you see?

Pretty soon we will all see Him. In the sky, soaring high, waiting on you and I. Can you see Him and me, or can you see you and He? Yes it must be me, me and you with Him, you see, living free eternally.

This poem was given to me through life experiences.

To Trust God

While life's disappointments stare you in the face, hold on tight, fight, and stay in the race.

In daily situations the things that you face want to knock you out of the race. Hold on tight and fight.

Trust in the Lord with all you've got, and fight a good fight of faith, for that same race just might keep you face-to-face with the Lord your God whom you trust in.

This poem, "Gently Urging Me," was given to me through a new level in God and how He communicates with me. I found out from self-experience that God is not going to force Himself on us, nor will He scream and shout at us. He has a very gentle way of getting our attention; it is so gentle that in a given moment, we may sometimes miss His communication. There are times when He allows us a second chance before we miss the moment of His direction to the way we should go. If we pay attention to His warning, it will save us some heartaches. It may also save gas and time spent on something that could have been avoided. Psalm 119:105 reads as follows: "Thy word is a lamp unto my feet, and a light unto my path."

Gently Urging Me

I feel the need to move forward. Although I think I know where I'm going, I feel the need. While traveling up the road, there is an urge to stop at the store. I feel the need. I totally ignored that gentle urge inside of me, and I continued on up the road. I feel the need. Instead I went to another store approximately thirty miles up the road. I feel the need. While I was at that store, I feel the need. I found out what I needed was at the first store. I feel the need. Now I know I should have stopped at the first store. I feel the need. I ignored the gentle urge warning me. I feel the need. Then I went nearly thirty miles back down the road to get what I wanted from the store. I really feel the need. Now I am somewhat relieved, for now I have the need.

This poem was God given to me after my mother became ill and I felt like I was going to lose her. A few days later, God delivered my mother and she is well. Hallelujah to the King of kings and the Lord of lords.

Softly Slipping Away

Here I sit, for I feel that your time is drawing nearer to be with God. My heart is not heavy, but my eyes are getting watery with tears. I can feel my chest getting full, and now I want to cry. Instead, I sigh because I think of the place where you are going. Softly slipping away. The more I watch you in the early morning hours, my inside groan. Oh how I'm going to miss you, for others have come and gone, but you, my dear, meant so much to me. What do we say? What shall we do? At this time, the only words I can say are thank you. We must remain strong, for I see you are softly slipping away, and here we must stay until another day. I am not going too moan because I know that you are going to a better place where Christ sits on the throne. So when it's your turn, kindly come on along, for I don't want you to miss going home.

ABOUT THE AUTHOR

I am the second oldest of seven children. I was conceived in Rochester, New York. My daddy, Earnest Eugene Roberts, was on his dying bed when he told my mother, Mary Frances Moore, that she was pregnant with me. He died at Highlander Hospital in Feburary1959 in New York. I was born October of the same year he died. I never knew much about him, and I only saw him in an old photograph that my aunt, Gladys Roberts, had given to my mother. To my knowledge, this is the reason why God has given me that gift to cure the thrush, for I have never seen my dad alive. This was told to me by Mrs. Rose Farmer after we moved to a small town called Patterson, GA. Later on Mrs. Rose became my second grandmother after the death of my grandmother.

I have a college degree in electronics technology-communication technology, with a grade point average of 3.3. The reason I chose electronics as my major was because I wanted to learn how to do trigonometry. Mathematics was my favorite subject. Actually, I wanted to be a mathematician. On July 5, 2005, I received a letter of achievement from C. Paul Scott, who was the president of Altamaha Technical College for my outstanding grade average of 4.0 during my spring quarter that year.

But God the Lord is the only one who can tear anything down and build it back better than it ever has been before, even if that thing has had a thorn in the flesh. I thank God for looking beyond my faults and seeing my needs. My experience in going to college was a great one, for I had good professors who were good motivators to me—Dr. Mostseller at Altamaha College and Dr. Marsha and Dr. Barbara at Brunswick College. I was failing in algebra my first semester until Dr. Barbara came to class with her great speech. She said, "Some of you are not going to make it." I took that speech very personally—not in a negative way, but a positive way and math became my main subject. The more problems I was able to solve, the more involved I became in algebra. At one point I was so involved in my math class that I was solving algebra problems in my dreams. I was dedicated to this class, for I was determined to pass. I didn't pass with honors, but most importantly, I passed the class. It is because of God given me a sound mind that I am, thankful to be able to have a second chance in life.

ACKNOWLEDGMENTS

This book is dedicated to the Roberts, Reynolds, Grants, Bryants, Jernigans, Milledges, Farmers, Smiths, Saddlers, Thomas's, Jones, Fussells, church family, enemies, and friends. To God be the glory.

CPSIA information can be obtained
at www.ICGtesting.com
Printed in the USA
BVHW022302180522
637376BV00002B/41